haiku to you
& *various mutterings*

Richard Seiberlich

Illustrated by
Emmie Pappa - 13 years old

My daughter and son-in-law, Gail and Dave, encouraged me to continue with this effort, and there were times when such encouragement was the difference between stop and go. So for better or worse this work is dedicated to them with my undying gratitude.

After Gail and Dave read, edited and made a few suggestions (which I adopted), Dave asked if I planned to include an introduction. I had not, but only because the thought never occurred to me.

So here it is.

When I was 21 years old, the army sent me to Korea following 14 weeks of infantry basic training in Kentucky during June, July and August 1951. Our route was from San Francisco by plane (4 propellers) to Tokyo, Japan with a refueling stop on Wake Island of World War II fame. In Tokyo we were put on a train for a two day trip to Sasebo, Japan, the southern port city across the water from Pusan, Korea. Sasebo was the replacement depot for the forces in Korea. As our group was preparing our newly-issued MI rifles and rolling our field packs for the "ferry" ride to Pusan, my name and two others were called. Upon reporting to the lieutenant I was informed I'd be remaining in Sasebo to fill a vacant spot for a typist in the Correspondence and Locator Section.

In addition to the academic courses in high school, I took a commercial course which included bookkeeping, shorthand (Pittman), and typing. Thus was I saved from combat and kept in Japan for the next 21 months. At this point I wish I could say I became immersed in Japanese culture, lifestyle, language, etc. Sadly, this was not the case. We worked from 8 to 5, five days a week, and except for an occasional updating with weapons training, the rest of the time was our own. We we were all just turned 20 or 21, and had an interset in booze, cigarettes, and Sasebo night life. The latter consisted of taxi dancers (10 cents a dance), and our favorite hangout was the "Kasbah". My knowledge of the language extended to the important situations, e.g. "You speak.....how much?" Or, "Hayako GI, MP's come". I learned to love sukiyaki with a raw egg on top, Japanese beer (Asahi), and the ladies. The men disliked us for many reasons, the principal one being that we spoiled their women by treating them like women. One example: the ladies were shocked when we insisted that they walk alongside us instead of the customary three or four paces behind as a sign of the man's superiority.

I don't recall ever reading or even hearing about Haiku all the months I was there. As a matter of fact I don't remember when I became interested in this form. Obviously I learned of it somewhere along the way, and enjoyed the discipline required to compose the verse.

For many years I've made notes of items of interest that I've heard, observed, or conceived in my own mind. The "Various Mutterings" section contains a goodly number of those items. Some date back years, while others could have been recorded a few days prior to the writing of this introduction (right now it's August 23, 2002).

Finally, Dave asked me what kind of audience was I trying to reach. The subject matter of both the Haiku and Mutterings would indicate an adult group. The Mutterings have "something for everyone," i.e. family types, male and female singles, lotharios, feminists, reasonably deep thinkers (not too deep), and even political types. If you happen to read the book and think of a category I've omitted, feel free to contact me and I'll happily add it to the sequel. How's that for optimism?

haiku – an unrhymed verse form of Japanese origin having three lines containing usually 5, 7 and 5 syllables respectively; also: a poem in this form usually having a seasonal reference.

Ergo...Haiku's not Haiku
Unless a season's cited.
Then Haiku's Haiku.

MUSIC!!!

Can't live without it. Whatta you mean, what do I mean? Every time I start to think life's boring and routine, along comes a new song to convince me that life is indeed worthwhile. Did you say, "...for example?" The first couple will reveal my age.

"Heartaches" by Ted Weems' orchestra with Elmo Tanner whistling.

"Volare" by ???

"There I've Said It Again" by Vaughn Monroe.

"Lucky Old Sun" By Frankie Lane.

"Something" (in the way she moves) by George Harrison and the Beatles.

"Crying" by Roy Orbison.

"Whiter Shade of Pale" by Procol Harum.

"Vincent" (Starry, starry night) by Don McLean.

"Eye in the Sky" by The Alan Parsons Project.

Just about anything by Hank Williams Senior,
George Jones, or Willie Nelson.
And this is just scratching the surface. I should have
included Leon Russell's "Back to the Island."
Not to mention Kiri Te Kanawa singing Richard Strauss's
"Four Last Songs;" any Puccini aria;
Wagner's "Love/Death" from Tristan und Isolde.
More oldies:
"Unchained Melody" original by Al Hibler.
"Blue Moon" by Billy Eckstine or Bob Dylan.
"You Belong to Me" by Jo Stafford.
"Soft Winds" by Dinah Washington.
Anything at all by Ella Fitzgerald and Patsy Cline

Again…Just scratching the surface.

Have the feeling no one's interested?

No one looks at you?

No one pays attention?

Get in the car and drive around until you see a house with a dog
on the porch; the dog will watch you.

Summertime. Dinner, a concert, back to the car and a Maria
Callas Tape.

The car our palace
As we listened to Callas
A Summer night's dream.

Go ahead. Count the syllables.

Sitting in the airport lounge reading a very tender part of the novel in which the couple is making love. He paused to digest the scene, and looked up to see an attractive woman smiling at him. His first reaction was egotistical. Then he realized that he had been smiling also as he looked up.

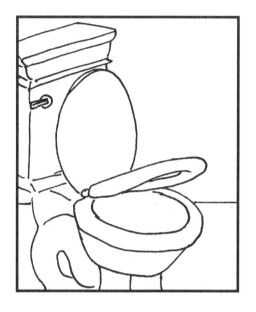

She: (After having sat on the cold porcelain part of the commode) "Why do you always leave the seat up?"

He: (following a pause) "Why do you always leave the seat down?"

She: (with a smile) "Well, I guess I'll never ask that question again."

They're still in bed late Sunday morning. Comes
the sound of distant drums from the high school band practicing
in the field. Then the church bells...nearer. Said one to the
other, "There's a study in contrast: the drums of war and the bells
of peace."

The one who flunked out of school is always the one to confront the young nephew, "You doin' good in school?" Like a threat.

"I don't take a good picture" translates into "They haven't yet made the camera capable of capturing my beauty."

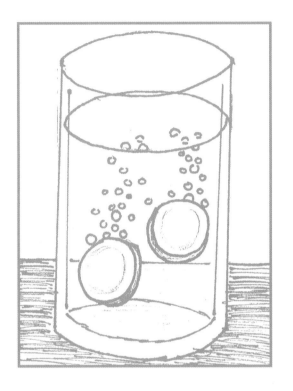

Her name was Hepsiba.

Upon hearing this, one of them laughed; the other one smiled and said it sounded like a relief for upset stomach.

You would present an idea, groping for the proper, descriptive adjective, finally offering a feeble substitute for what you couldn't remember. And then quietly, promptly, he would exercise his advantage and supply the right word.

They are in love but not yet together.

Snow to water now,
The promise of Spring is change.
We must join somehow.

He allowed that the salad looked tired.

"In fact," he said, "it looked as though it were tired even before it took the trip from the kitchen."

He had the look of a man whose back was in constant need of scratching.

Hoping to end the debate, he proclaimed, "Hemingway was not a shallow writer, but his writing was shallow."

Watching then president Clinton fence with the special prosecutor on television, it occurred to me that confronting him with the truth was much like confronting a vampire with a cross, but with one significant difference; the vampire had the decency to withdraw.

She: He doesn't like being with people smarter than he is.

He: Oh? In other words, he doesn't like being with most people.

It's Spring, all is right,
My thoughts of her suit the time.

They are fresh and bright.

He: Can you read that?

She: No.

He: That's good to know because I can't read it either.

She: Did you ever stop to think that we both might need glasses?

What do you mean the people in this country are not resourceful? Just remember, the people in this country learned to open the milk carton!

He: (upon reading her memoir) It's dull. Not interesting.

She: I hope you don't labor under the illusion that everything
        you say is like a Samuel Johnson quote.

After a late night cup of coffee, they said goodnight, each going off in his and her car. Unbeknownst to him, she on an impulse, followed him home. He was pleasantly surprised and certainly touched. After they went inside, he excused himself, went into his home office, and ten minutes later emerged with the following:

> She appeared, seemingly out of nowhere,
> In the dark of the night.
> And then the dark was gone.
> The love in her eyes provided light.
> The stars were impressed.

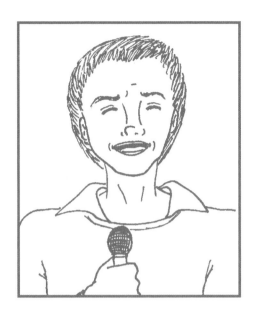

He was trying to explain why "worry is a wasted emotion," that it changes nothing. He said, "It's kinda like listening to Joe Cocker sing "You Are So Beautiful" for the first time. I was shocked at the obviously strained effort he needed to reach that final note.

Then when I heard it another time, I found myself instinctively worrying for him...even though I realized he had to make it because it was a recording."

Trying to overcome his reputation for being a heartless entrepreneur interested only in the bottom line, his speech was filled with kindness and platitudes. But one member in the audience couldn't help leaning into the ear of his companion and whisper, "Beneath that veneer of civility beats a heart of plutonium."

Whither this weather?
    Hey! Summer brings fruit from buds.

                Phooey on flash floods.

What's happening?

And whom are you blaming for it?

He was the kind of guy who was uncomfortable ordering just a cup of coffee in a restaurant; he'd also order an unwanted bagel or muffin. Insecure?

He greeted his chore with as much anticipation as he had shown when preparing to sit on a toilet seat in a cold barracks on January mornings in Minnesota.

"Real People' TV show to Blackstone, Jr. the magician:
"Do you think your father is watching you perform?"
Reply: "I hope so." Not an answer to the question.

He was attempting to make a comparison and came up with this: "It's like listening to an opera in English. Or the Mass being sung in English. Not the same. No mystery. Did you ever hear a good opera in English? Hell no!"

He: Are you implying that I am lying?

She: No, but I've inferred that you have erred.

I forgive you for not forgiving me.

She sleeps by my side
As the moon watches Autumn,
Then home she must ride.

He: So and so called in sick.

She: Takes a lot to keep him out.

He: Yeah. About 2 quarts of gin.

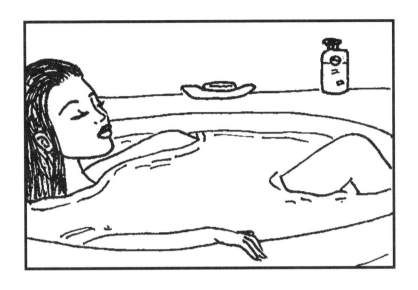

She: Last night I was ruminating in the bath tub.

He: Well, I hope you cleaned it up.

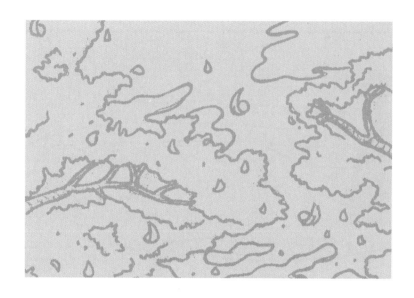

The leaves are falling.
'Tis earth's autumnal calling.
Are we there to hear?

She was wearing a yellow rain slicker with matching
rain hat.

"You look very nautical," he said. "Where do you keep your
ship...
or hasn't it come in yet?"

He was so not with it that he made requests of progressive jazz groups back in the '50's.

The profound type: One of his biggest goals in life was
keeping his sideburns balanced.

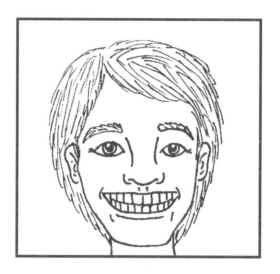

His smile was the kind of a smile that invited a punch in the mouth.

A Short Scene

He: Kiss me.

She: Just like that? Kiss me? Can't you at least put some feeling into the idea? You make it sound like an order: "Kiss me!!"

He: Why must you always complicate everything? It wasn't an order. It was the beginning of what I hoped would develop into a great result.

She: Well let me inform you that you definitely lack the needed charm, panache, whatever, and that you can go and kiss...............

He: (interrupting) Hold it! I refuse to let you desecrate the beauty that I associate with that word. I can't help you and your interpretations, but I use "kiss" in truly romantic terms, and I have only romantic intentions. Understand how seriously I feel about this. Please!

She: ....my ass!

See her enduring.
But a new Spring in nearing.
Now she's endearing.

One thing about old people....when you call, they're usually at home.

He was watching a ballet on the Bravo channel.

"You sure can't afford to have ingrown toenails, can you?"

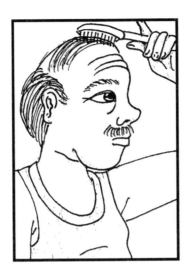

Meticulous? He was as meticulous as a balding man arranging those last, precious hairs over and around the ever-expanding area to be covered up.

She dances with ease,
Bringing joy like endless Springs.

Her feet could be wings.

He promised her that he wouldn't see his ex anymore, but he had to return the car. She followed in hers to bring him back. He entered his ex's house with the keys and returned in 15 minutes.

She: That took you long enough to just return the keys. Are you sure you aren't going to see her anymore?

He: I don't know.

She: But I thought you said...................

He: (interrupting) I don't know. Leave me alone with it. OK??

She: I'll leave you alone with everything (wondering if he caught her meaning).

TV scene from Public TV documentary: An eagle
fighting off intruders after the eggs in its nest. My then six year
old daughter watching the constant battle finally asks, "Doesn't
anybody just come to visit?"

We walk and we talk,
Watching as the snowflakes swarm.

She makes Winter warm.

Not to be confused with Haiku

I lie here entranced,
My feelings for her enhanced.
Such is her touch.

The following was inspired by her phone call urging
him to view the crescent moon.

"Look at my most favorite moon" said she.
So...look at her most favorite moon did he.
On an invisible chain hung this glowing crescent,
Gracing the neck of the indigo sky.
A diamond, when compared, proved evanescent.
"She caused this" said he. How lucky am I."

While dancing..............
Her upswept tress, her Gauguin dress,
Her lyrical voice to songs of her choice,
Her "following" feet....poetry in motion.
All this inspired a happy devotion.

What's wrong with applauding after the first, second or third movement of a great symphony? I've done it impulsively (to acute embarrassment).

March 28, 2002. Sid Caesar and Alan King were on PBS's "The News Hour with Jim Lehrer" remembering Milton Berle who'd just died. Caesar's "Your Show of Shows" was (is) an icon of television, or any other form of comedy. Sid has lost too much weight and gained too much age to be appearing with his hair so scraggly and his beard unfulfilled. Alan King was a study in contrast with his clean shaven face and closely trimmed hair.

Give me an example of survival instinct.

OK, you're driving a car and engaging in heated conversation at the same time. You look at your passenger to emphasize points, but your survival instinct tells you when to look back to the road.

I venture forth upon the path,
Knowing not the aftermath.
But going out I have a hunch

If I'm not careful, I'll catch my lunch.

He had the trained eye of a scavenger working the roadside from a bicycle.

I've seen and (simultaneously) heard many high school teenagers speeding in cars with the radio blaring, a manifestation of their indifference to their roadway surroundings. Recently I witnessed a teenager being helped from the wreckage of a car. His expression was a mixture of horror, disbelief, and above all, fright, In just one instant that cocky, cool character, unconcerned about others' safety, became a believer. That was the look I saw.

February 26, 2002....The Wall Street Journal had an article about Senator Robert Torricelli's alleged acceptance of illegal gifts from a Mr. Chang. The case had been turned over to the Senate Ethics committee by the outgoing U.S. attorney. One of the senator's remarks was reminiscent of Bill Clinton's reply to Jim Lehrer's question during an interview on Public Television at the height of the Monica Lewinsky affair. Mr. Lehrer asked the then president if he had a relationship with Ms. Lewinsky. Mr. Clinton's famous response was something like "There is no relationship." Surprisingly, Mr. Lehrer let it go instead of saying, "OK, but was there one?"

Senator Torricelli's answer to a question about having received gifts was "There were not gifts exchanged." He wasn't asked if gifts were exchanged; he was asked if gifts were ever received. Yet there was no challenge to his obviously improper response.

Am I going deaf, or do you also find the dialogue in today's movies and television shows to be inaudible?

During one of his recent shows of "The O'Reillly Factor,"
Bill O"Reilly said, "The powerful protect each other," or words
to that effect. He's right.

Has anyone ever told the American people (politicians love to refer to "the American people") about the pension plan that is in effect for the Congress? Although uninformed, I have heard it's pretty generous. Is a copy of the plan available for the American people to review?

When I saw her, I thought I could love her.
When I touched her, I knew I could love her.

When I knew her, I loved her.

He was the kind of guy who, in a conversation, felt it necessary to refer to Elvis as Elvis Presley.

When I wrote this, I was thinking of Sammy Davis, Jr.
performing with Sinatra, et al.

They see me walk, they hear me talk,
The watch me shimmy and shake.
"What about the crowd?" you ask.
And I say, "Let them eat cake."
(thank you Marie Antoinette)

Inscrutable Asian? Horse feathers. They're just as capable of wearing emotion on their sleeve as I am. Especially when it comes to crying.

I tend to attach too much credibility, too much impor-
tance, too much success to the other person. But it's a positive
tendency. However, whenever that person(s) disappoints or
deceives me, I figuratively shake my head and wonder when this
gullibility will cease.

Her laugh matched her face.
Vibrant as an Autumn breeze.
She exuded grace.

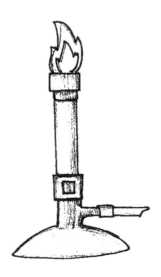

He: Let's do it.

She: I don't feel any chemistry between us.

He: You can't have any chemistry until you light the Bunsen burner.

Begin with a belief. Not an assumption. Not a hope. But a belief.

In "Saving Private Ryan" and HBO's special series on a regiment of the 101st Airborne Division, both dealing with the Normandy invasion and subsequent battle inland, the weapons disparity was incredible. Most of the time our guys were fighting with the venerable M1 rifle against the enemy's machine guns, mortars, and artillery. I never understood this.

While watching Kurt Masur conduct the orchestra in
Richard Strauss' "Don Juan, Opus 20" on public TV, he became
preoccupied with trying to count the buttons on Masur's
foresleeve. Later he smiled when he decided that Strauss would
not have been amused.

Willard Muggins once told me as we were driving to Baltimore from Philadelphia, "Every so-called "free" piece of sex cost me an average of $43.25." And bear in mind he said this in 1958 when, as the saying goes, a dollar was a dollar. But Willard's sense of humor deserted him one night when, at the age of 53, he jumped from the 28th floor where, we were to learn, his psychiatrist had an office. I say "learn" because none of his associates were aware of this therapy.

He #1: Doesn't it make you sad not being remarried,
          being alone?

He #2: I assure you of two things. First, I am never alone
          in the sense of the word. Second, my moments of
          sadness are far, far fewer than your moments of regret
          and frustration.

He #1: Oh.

Though winter must come,
I think not about its cold.

My warmth is in you.

I subscribed to Newsweek magazine which, as I understand it, should be delivered every Monday. It rarely reaches my mailbox before Wednesday, and Thursday has become the norm. Imagine my surprise when I heard Don Imus, whom I watch on MSNBC cable, mention on a Monday morning that he was reading his copy of Newsweek which is delivered to his residence on Sunday evening. Now that I think about it, he does have Howard Fineman and Jonathan Alter (Newsweek journalists) on his program; maybe they make the delivery.

Probably my best friend (I've known him for 30 years) is Mike Eddy who is regarded, among our little group, as poet laureate, i.e. he will compose a couple of verses for any occasion, and more often than not they are deliberately and hilariously offensive. Well, it's payback time.

> There once was a man named Eddy
> Whose demeanor was more than unsteady.
> With offensive lines he harassed his friends,
> Till he blew up and died from the bends.

Actually, he still lives a very active life, and still finds time to wax poetic when called for.

I have another best friend (it's possible to have two best friends if you ignore the grammatical aspect) Neil Mahlstedt whom I've also known for 30 years. He and I are of Irish/German descent and could be related on the Irish side: his ancestors were O'Kane and mine were Kane. Anyway, Neil has both a great sense of humor and what I call a false "bad" temper. One night a group of us were at dinner and seated at another table were some women, familiar and unfamiliar. I gave a collective greeting to them. Neil elected to say "hello" to one of the familiar whose name he'd forgotten. He leaned over to me and asked, "What's her name?" I couldn't resist the mischief and told him it was Jane. He smiled and said, "Hi Jane." She gave him a cold look and said, "My name's not Jane, it's Marie." Neil was not amused, but the rest of us had a good laugh. Six weeks later, believe it or not, we all were at the same restaurant and at the next table was a group of women all of whom we knew. Talk about deja vu. I greeted them after which Neil whispered to me, " What's the second one on the left's name?" I could not suppress a silly grin revealing my intent whereupon his false "bad" temper came into play when he hissed, "Don't f— with me Richard!!" A laugh riot ensued.

They were seated next to each other at a wedding reception dinner. She was an older woman whose husband was out of the country on business. Since they had never met before, he decided that books would be an innocuous subject for conversation. She was indeed an avid reader of books, so he proceeded with what he considered an appropriate next step....he asked how many tomes were in her library. Her answer surprised him. "I discard them or give them away. Why on earth would you want to keep a book?" Caught completely off guard, he retreated to silence by keeping his mouth occupied with the dinner before him until he could think of a response to such a disagreeable position.

Now he was ready. "Would you disown your children after raising them?" "Of course not," she replied. "Well there!!" he yelped, with a self-satisfied grin. "If I read a book, it becomes my child!" She couldn't wait to get out of there.

Attempt at humor in a haiku.

"Let's boogie," said he.
"It is Summer and it's hot,"
Said she. "I think not."

A CEO"s message to company employees: "There will be more layoffs that will be not insubstantial." What's wrong with saying, "There will be more substantial layoffs."? The former statement could be a tip-off of the individual's mind set which, in turn, tells why there will indeed be more layoffs.

May 9, 2002. I watched a documentary on The Learning Channel titled, simply, "Gulag." It depicted life (if you can call it that) in the notorious Russian prison camps, as well as how quickly, and unjustly, a citizen could end up there. They were used as slave labor in the various industries connected with the prisons. And this was the major cause for being arrested; the need for laborers. Conditions were inhuman. The surprising part was that some prisoners actually survived to confirm their nightmarish existences. This was life under the communist system as dictated by Lenin, then Stalin and their thugs. I was stunned at the cruelty. How could anyone defend or justify a form of government that permitted, actually created, such abuse?

All of this reminded me of an Academy Awards ceremony a few years ago which included a special award to the famous, aging stage and film director Elia Kazan. There were some dissenters. Seems Mr. Kazan, in his youth, became a member of the American communist party. But after a period of time he (in my opinion) demonstrated his perspicacity by becoming disillusioned with this party and he resigned. Hopefully, his decision was influenced by the communist party's ultimate goal, viz. the overthrow of the government of the United States of America.

Among the dissenters were two very talented Hollywood actors Nick Nolte and Ed Harris. After his departure from the communist party, Mr. Kazan was called upon by the U.S. Congress to reveal the names of any members of the party with whom he had been acquainted. He cooperated. Evidently the Messrs. Nolte and Harris disrespected him for his decision to be an informer. Mr. Kazan had knowledge of the party's ulterior motives which was more than enough for him to convey all the names possible. Far from being a "squealer" or "rat," Elia Kazan is a hero for his decision. There is definite irony in the conduct of the Messrs. Nolte and Harris. When the special "Oscar" was presented, Mr. Kazan was greeted with a standing ovation from an audience of some 3,000. Except for the Messrs. Nolte and Harris; they remained seated.....on their hands. I was embarrassed for them. They looked like two petulant children. And the irony? Had the communists succeeded in taking over our country, the likes of the Messrs. Nolte and Harris would have ended up in a gulag!!